FILIAL ARCADE AND OTHER POEMS.

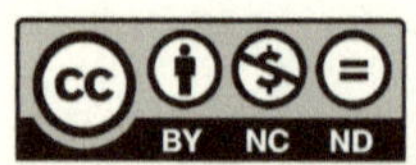

printed by lightning source, milton keynes
in an endless edition (version 131221)
ISBN 978-94-91914-00-3

uitgeverij, den haag
shtëpia botuese, tiranë
editore, firenze
出版社, singapore

www.uitgeverij.cc

A. STALEY GROVES,

Filial Arcade & Other Poems.

IMAGES BY MARCO MAZZI.

:

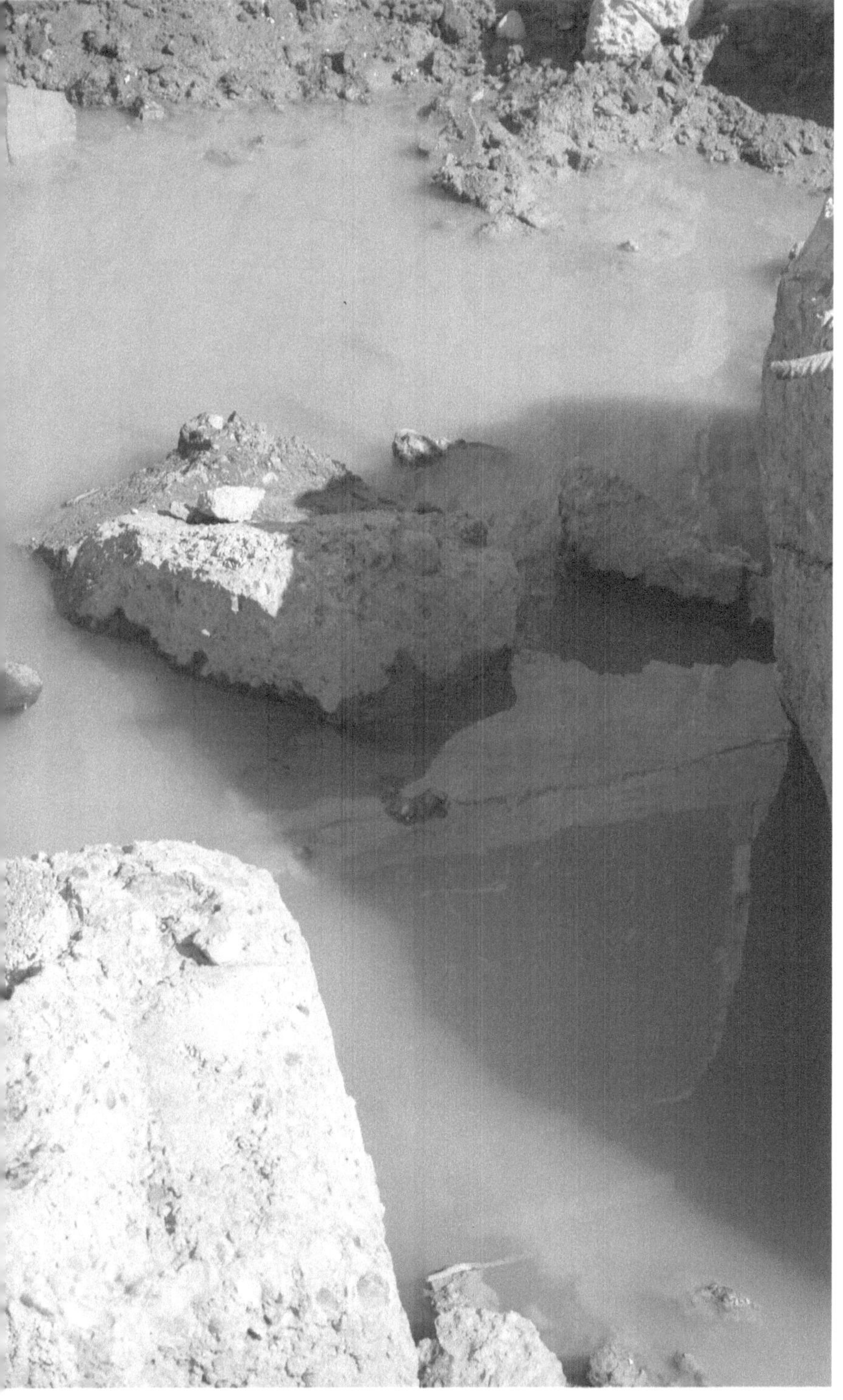

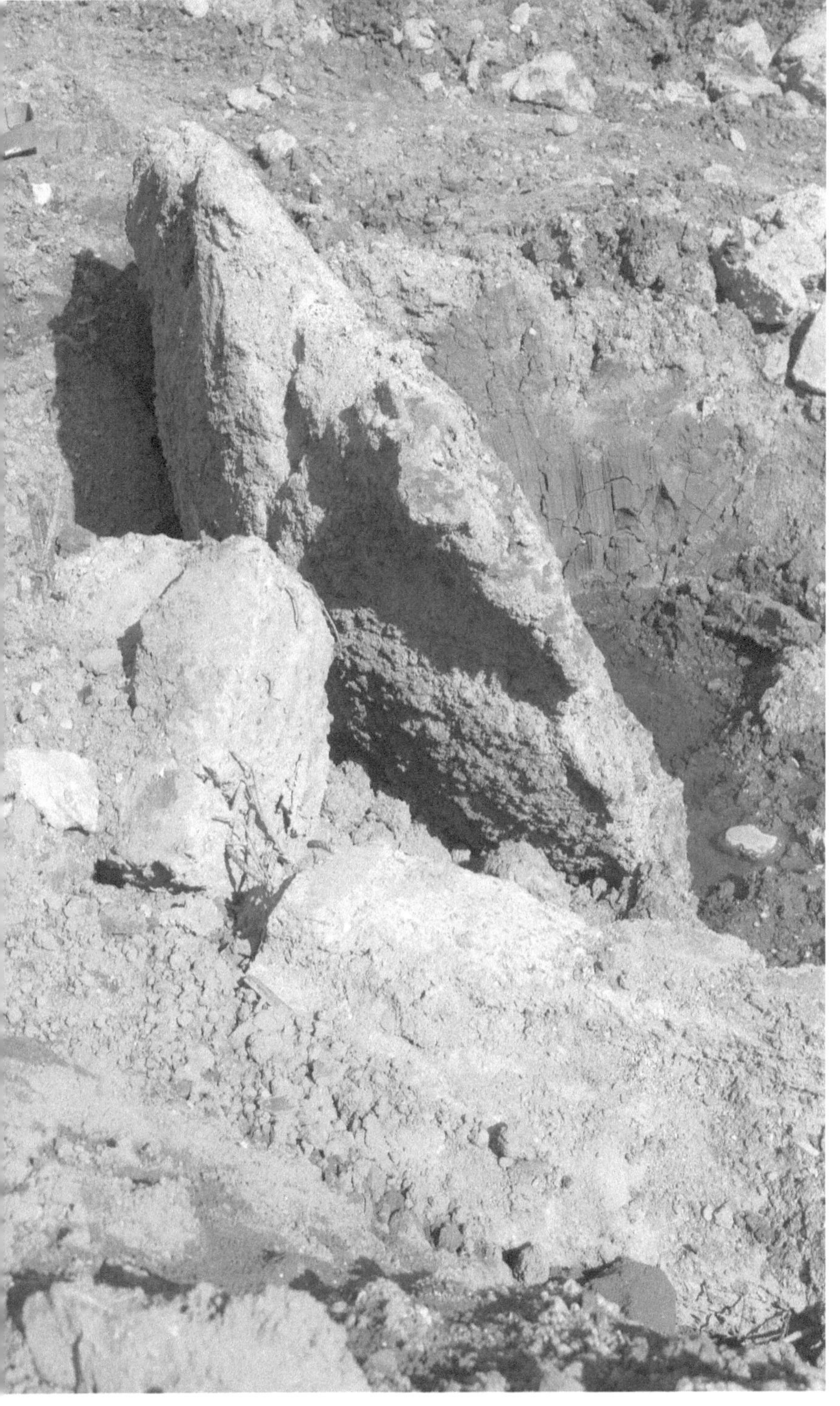

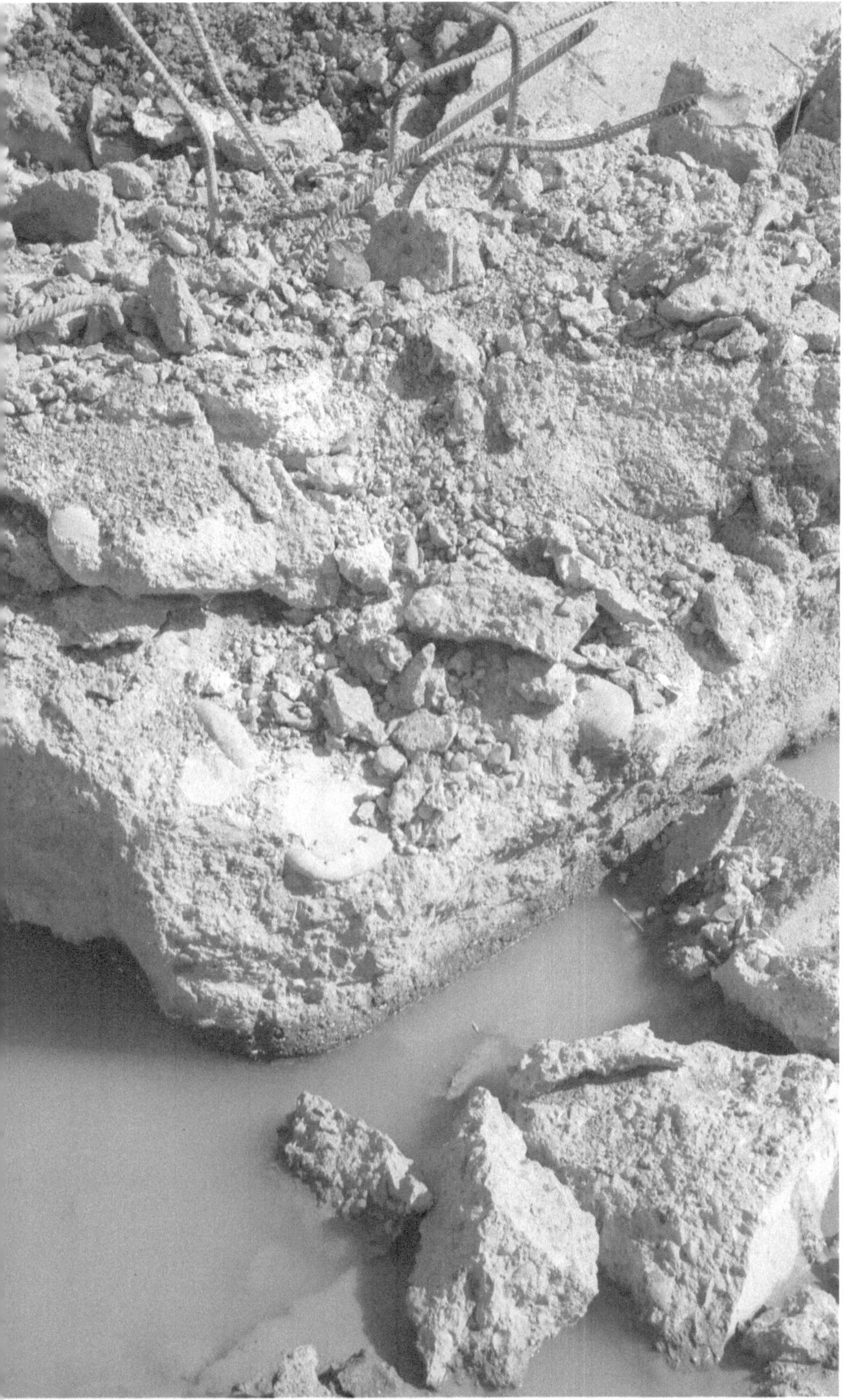

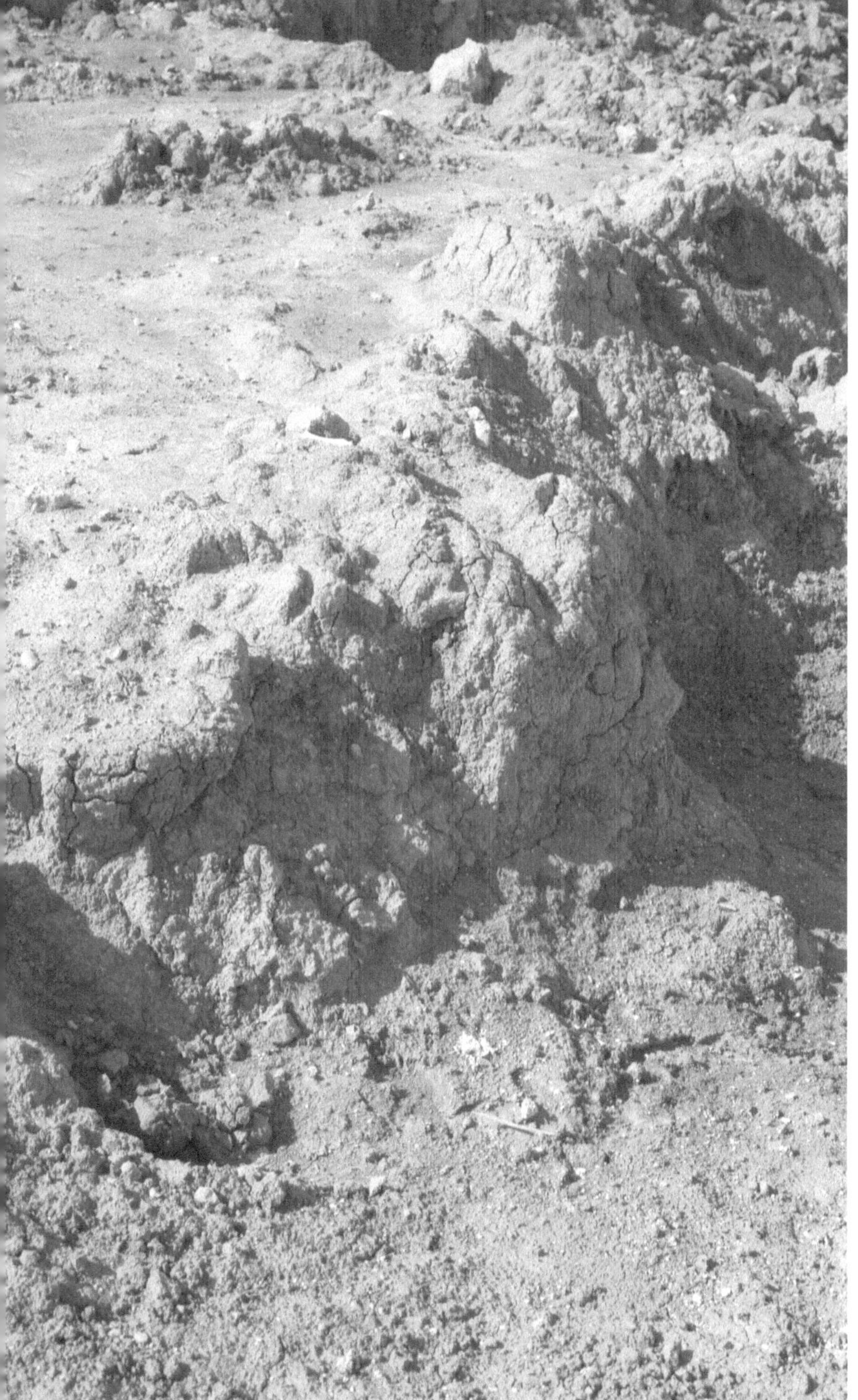

For Robs,
see you at Big Splash.

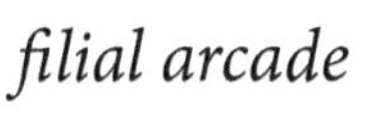

filial arcade

1

stars
pult apart
obsidian earth eyes with stars?

pulls apart slow mouth
desire circles in lungs
the

de- sidus
ex- sidiuos

did not realize
such a drive

the presence of a naked body.
wants taken in.
to find peace.
to be buried.
feelings obscure in expression
star face scrawled in scars,
or pult apart in stars.
longed to shown,
in this world,
the face there.

as there have been others,
who wrote
hierophant figures there,
  beyond expression here.

mapping the intelligence of a palm

the fingers gentle
a grasshopper's antennae
a finger
slips, behind the neck
a finger
rest, in the old brain
the finger taps, brain stars

spider hand opens the wings of the
old brain
the wrist.
...

the instructions of the hand
the unspelt
the
water in the hand
the respite
the water gone black.

the breath circles the lungs
the obsidian circles with stars
pulls apart the lips.

the unlearning of thinking in the kiss
beyond milk, beyond
...

do not waste a kiss
do not kiss a frog
do not kiss the king
nor his daughter
kiss from the soil

soil
where ancestors are pulled apart

soil that's full of feet, hands, faces, plants
and that man who fills a bottomless shoe
do not kiss him.

kiss from the soil the soil
through all bodies
until mud fills your lungs
and vapors populate
all empty homes
until homes smelting in obsidian soil
...

kiss from the soil to soil
until the hands become water
wrist become silk
until the milk runs thin in bloods
until the tree pulls out of all chests
as incredulous inertia
an incredulish great machinery
wrapped in birdbrains.

Sealung Persafon
you wrapped your tongue
around my voice,
showing perhaps
worlds in permeating
silence.
a flushish permeation
collecting
silences,
aspects of speaking.

stare at water
slow lumplungs in the inlet
like I dropped something
from the silence of thought;
in speaking.
my tongue cannot collect
silences dropped
into the water:

murky now sad
now visible now
missing.
...

Iris means roar eyes and
blink *per-* of an annual, concomitant spectacle;
roar whorls behind
and intersects
a flush aspect of eyes,
same say for lushlish
sea pulse
water.
Iridous
colorlungs came, said,
my tongue to
my thought: aspect spect
...

take an edge like moss.
as a hierofigure, observed moss on concrete
or algae on mortar, on bricks.
the sealung,
the colorlungs, a surface of
dropped silences.
seacilia grasps with triumphant limpness
the hierophantic mother
seafieldsun.

hand oar of a childish tree
yet deep slumber
tucked in
silent bellows.
at times passes through
  eyes,
at times voice.

one imagines, no different than;
came breath in the lungs
that; strums vocal chords
where; lettering meets bellown-ing.
sent from a spine
wraps round square language.

no different:
the sea a flag and sun sets
mild tide curve.
does not crest.
  blue gives way
and passes through

the lungs and irides,
iridious laughter
quiet us.
...

the deep roar is silence
and to call it a roar
to recall an oar breaks water.
the children abandoned,
sunken slaves still sink still,
the sun breaks parts colors
sets, brings blue;
  travels sun among salt.

the sea children on,
paeon on shoreline palms,
weaving wove hats
children sing sea face color.

the children, tidal ovulation
tones impatient circle
whorl hats,

the roar is silent
the oar a child's handling smile.
child squats
a living shadow at dusk
against the sun.

the palms woven, roarwhorl
slow wind,
the children call back their shadows,
the shadow hand oars slow crest.
…

on the balcony
the horizon
silence fills up color.

  still looking
at that water, there then silence:
'logic' of the smile
in eyes and voice.

a bellow if,
Mercurial roar sets,
what's seen breaking,
pulled under the world,
where slaves sink and children blink
up in breaks,
pulse of squatted shadows
rolling over.

When looking out from the balcony,
    behind in plain view
your sandals in the sand
fingers trace the hands.
palm sky
the green fury of spring storms lost,
eternal summer,
no fall

vastish palp + palm,
shake touch
wonder what it meant.
to who, whom. suckle aspects, each season.

rather than objects in front of them,
or what they demand be in front of them,
as if the will.
and then, missing afar, more stunning.
dead life of fixed targets:
all lush, poverty
vacuous, may, be, near colorful,
or delicate, fine gentle shake touch
behind morereal
reality.
...

fingers sink into hot palm,
palpates of the water
heat sank into the green storm sky
liquified loverly, Mercury passed
this ex loqui
. . .

and sight not seeing moves in
the waking dithyramb, event of lovers
not tragic, iridious written
'older than the ancient world'
not godly.
  there no object to,
father founding moments are
still at hand moving fingers into palm,
in the pulse of passage
florid, amphibulous shake swollen
this inverse tonguing, reads my mind,
takes up aspects, tongue in cheek
...

a worm digs in soil.
peeks between your sandalless toes
turns earth, a mercuriality.
and read it back to
still hand at hand still fingers sink
outside of common sense.
trace the fragments of footfellings
in palms,
back of the neck
on paths passing.

wanted mythology
finally mythopoeia to
wonder wanderlingering.

orbit of oak
and even the knees
remind me, soaked by your silk hands,
instilling washes without volume.

recalled: once sitting in the oak tree
seen the leaf stem, worn, yellow, languid
flecklish.

you cannot help me?
this life folded in, pult
around or among
aspects.
your nons-, amazing floridations
it is as is it

seen me in the tree then
lay in the wind
thoughts. the axiom the maxim
in all the oak trees.
  childhood trestles, the roots of the mind.
falling from the tree
crushed ankles.

from tree to tree the tree changes
whorl walking through antlers
the afternoon orbit.

my ribs stand up the tree
roots. the traffic of ants and bird droppings bespeckle
them. my boots are in the earth
.

2

gates are open
The gates always open
at the guard house
that hold them there.

stone wilting blossoms
dropped images sag on urns.

runs old oaks
on worn stone,
ventate shadows,
hand prints
of old oaks
root sky, ediface embossed.

fragment light
an ice sealing,
blinkt rainbow spectrum
comes fertile kernel sun.

a light bulb in the guard house hangs,
and handbranched
dawning sky
lays down on the window.
the guard sleeps.

gravel, asphault
rolls under foot
as chewing spines
of canned fish.

yesterday read headstones,
made an ignoble ambit.
at dawn watch the house.

nothing moves.
or orbitual wetness
moves and, moving again
a memory of walking
and the walking in the memory of noon.

humid dust of leaves, leaf dust
pressed down dawn
condensation
sucked up in breath,
caught in cillia
blown out in steam.
  chromantic quilt in the blubs singly roar.
regalia of the blinking mute,
  blinking color.
. . .

my mouth open to the east,
water lit water singly
  murmur on sea, a crownish
westend telegraph, a
vocated ice peacock,
opens sea singly.

light in the guard house
guards
the thoughtless typewritten
headstones.

my ears are at the end
of a water worn
light out on the water,
where treebranches finger final night stars.
...

the gate is open,
enter
the index of graves,
a closed up program
not talking about itself,
nor its paths.

we orbit dead pages of
emotional charges
reminds us, blown singly in wetness, what we don't
know about a poem paeon.

hands of our pour age:
drunks of night,
old drunk's days ahead.
pull on themselves,
each other, when wenches become virtuous, for
example,
when banal insecurities fall away
and somehow a human speaks
and for any moment it does, it speaks in anger.

recall: oak scent means the night's drunk with
                                        waterlush air, past that an
oak slime, caught on grass.
...

the trees palm the air,
hands-off, oak's hands,
roots; oak oars earth,
one hand in soil,
other in air.
hand in the pour age of a night,
oak hands off its hands, palpates sky.

the heart crowned by ribs, opens bulbously
umbilically to a westend sea singly.
aspects of the sea,
populates clouds sun comes kernel.
…

recall: wind flooded Ascension Parish
thought: doorways on the ground
and the pebbles
ladders
trinkets
gravetablets.

a sun cooked wind,
blows warm, in the warm
a cold
  that wrings faces.
winter blossoms.

the cold inside cheeks
the fleshish autumnal palms
dry up,
the oak full of singly
oaroara
:

dust dusk dons on
slime oak smelling night,
dons, the oblong passage
  pult particles of
memroar.

palms fall fold back
clap the world top to bottomworld
together.

the left right traffic in hands
  sea in the tree trunk
full of pressure, crowned by trestles
or a rolled up secreting sentence —
along all, along here:
on a singly, bulbous
  lighted water.

roaroaroak tree expresses like ears new clouds
tree palm leaves
the flesh fingers palms palpates mosses.
the peacock in the fall tree sings.
of fall leaves
brittle stems.
...

the tendons of the wrist
as a drive shaft, or elbow
stems and crooked fingers:
the dead attenuate
  night stylus.
insinuate roots.

in pour ages:
impoverished stones of the guard house
passers by
hoods engulf,
hoods severe heads,
from eye to eye punctuation.
...

my ankles need shoes,
keep walking to fathers
  mortified heroes
my toes buckle.
the bovine nose
  memoroar,
squareshovel oars
scent of silage, shoveled into buckets
a gruff exhale
the steam of bacteria.

  ankles in the hands of father mud,
walk in, attenuate styl-us.

a urine beam was
steaming in the night.
recall: walking across the gravel
teeth rolling under boots.
sitting on the bench.
your knees now need shoes.
  pallid beef tongue sunset.

suns up, broken circles
concentric earing
ringing ears
and
my belly walks,
a sleepy ground
think underground
  a nightsky space,
starry eyes of night blink back.

float my stomach through
night porridge of people,
  mud and skeletons
  sound lost soil,
slow shipwreck of a city dump dumping into itself.
drifting soil, the dead reposed as crumpling dignity.
my stomach full of sloops
vent house of soil
my belly button, open, breathing up
and filling the sentence tracts and homes with smelt.

there then the ribs
and the heart
we walk through the yard.
  by the guard house
the gate is open.

the ribs do not crown the heart
rather bones of wings
and the mud pours out
  encircling
pacer of an ear path

the heart laid a path
engines the mud,
a mud vent the stomach sails
sloopulous
heart path.
prints itself into the foot
and the crown that was
the ears of the tree
the flesh in autumn
  lexicon, rather etymologue. .

my autumn
there, old fathers express
feelings face
throats and veins,
on their old boots

and feathers found in the air
of the women who cast them up and off
the little hearts shot out of the sky
it snows now.

georgian language
fruit quivers
engorgeous

blossoms flop down
purple,
powder up the concrete path
flaps bounce.

the heart full of syrup
engorgroues fruit
in georgian.

farmer, from the land of wolves
or augustian engorgeous
peaches.
. . .

his lover was said to live there,
she was in there in alaska
the mental map, a scene lost to us.

when the sunlight went through their eyes
on a cruise, stylus memoar
unfolded.
the slown shattered snow stones
the ciclic prickle of a setting image,
dessicates.

her the next of a sequence
the part of the grand mother.

_ was born from her,
engore-ged
stamens of the blossom,
georgious.
antennae of the uterus, center of laughter,
o'various.
elbows of the arms
holding up grand mothers heart

ovaries
full
of oocyte
particles of a stone.

grand father, whose life is in the slug who
arches his back and
drags up the particles
and exhausts.

the cold mud boils
the fingers of the ground type into itself
the cyotee quick steps.
…

the fruit slips it syrup
from the stone heart of a peach
a bark center,
holds the slugs slow pressure well

the slug crawls through the tree
his serum.

the slug wears ovaries
to see through.

the slug watery stone pebbles
the same like the concreek bed
the clean if water
the old farm stream
that golden fabric of the many mini cresticulars
the gorge full of mucus
pure paper

the open mouth, the lips, the slugs fat bodies of the
mouth
the golden fabric busts up
rolling thick drops
drinking up
the pure papesse,
the face full of gold,
the stomach full of sandpebbles,

as an embering log
exploded
the face full of gold
the lips rubbing on another on
. . .

I am so far from you
time time time
the acres sat here

mythology of parental memories
he still sits there
hearing, perhaps, spines of frozen fish snap
watching the footprint freeze

there are no mirrors in this place
the memory a thick mucus
dessication it's threat of development
the brain
the slug human
genus, generous, gorgeousness
georgiousness
oocytation.

the human universe
burns up in the heart
held up by hands
the head in the sand
the head
a stomach
the eyes
never say anything
but what the blossom of the face tucks up around

them
the eyes dessicate

of the things we lived
the burning ooctations
the occult occasions

walking around on the elbows
sucking dry the lips
the young face drinking from the creek
the young child digesting itself
the deer's slug tongue on a salt block

the deer run,
the deer are rank
the deer run to the gun
like a child to a cliff.
the deer are broken
the deer stood at the top of the building
the deer eyes stood
like two elbows in the mud
the deer sees nothing

the deer hears nothing but phantom trees,
smells nothing but its conviction of the smell.
the smell is a thing,
the deer are splattered,

like blossoms.
on iowa hiways and interstates.
the whole city of their bodies.
turn dry purple, the guts.

deer stand, the light in their eyes
they see a phantom tree.

invaginate
the cotton ruffle drapes
and croak chorus frogs set the ruffle

the dreams were being read.
face of a woman
as was seen, black and white
over and over
again, even a face one does not
remember.
was seen as shame.

the day chat
was an entire seen still unseen
watching dreams what we do.

repulse popular polar
throttle of the glass jar rings.
the grasshopper in the frogs mouth.

hatred in the front seat
the trauma of a steering wheel
the gravel of the runner's ovular track.

false mommies
the smell of cut grass
the clumping mulch
the crabapple stone
thrown from the mower blade

the grand mother's
drapping arms skin.
the indians, on the blanket
the indian shooting a star
as if he needed to.

candy corn
the smell of breasts.
...

the sea is in this air, the vast is vasting
the stomach full of ruin
everyday ruins
the opaque sense.

the opaque dissonance sense
the unlearing
the collapse of dissonance
the clearling copper
the thick purpular
the way water slateglass
the eyes are opened
the opaque dissonance
the purpular clearling

the cocked bird in the loom of a
set of plates opaque plates let
the bird in the steel walkway runner.
the burd works its way in the loom.

the cocking bird
the cooking duck neck
the aural lift.
the blue snowing
closed eyes
the opaque sheer.
...

the Notion is the stomach
metabole
super and sub ordinary
tract
digest the orbit of the pressed dead ground

the opaque plates dissonant
and the purple bloon
and black partridge pierce the loom
entropemental loom
the black partridge
opens up the ground
and flies up fills files
...

the stomach waves like a flag in warm weather
this symbolic flame
the flag is the whole sea
in each cresticulation opening
the breaking sea
the sea contingency.
consciousness,
the octopus eye
among invaginated ruffles.

moves as a disintegrating tissue.
the tissues soaked light shadow of the partridge.

grand mother's arms
the skirt, drapes
metal rimmed kitchen table, like life.
the window is open, the spring skates the curtain
candy corn
in the jar,
bullfrogs
in the tank,
the mystical astrologer
on the hill.
the oak floor
the octopus' eyelid, invaginate camera
fireflies fill the jar.

the oak floor, filled with sunlight
soaked, burned in orange in amber
holds the pollen of ninety springs,
the summer lush grass cut and mown,
the dust of autumnal oak leaves, the butchery of winter
once loved.
the sunlight crown on opaque plates
let
the purpular bruise
the deep oxygen of thought
full of salt
block crystals
glint in the loom.

settle into the stomach,
thoughts of the ground
settle into breasts,
of the invaginated chest
where the heart blinks
as octopus beaks
make their call,
gently shifting tissues
in the skull
glinting with,
little transmitters.

write it into a loom
pen it;
hear the loon
whirl it tight
hear the octopus call the loon back
hear you calling back.

sitting in the bathroom.
the frosted windows.
the opaque dissonance of plates.
these images.
...

I am not lost but found it in
just as your hands remained when the partridge took up
put their horseshoes
in the air
as a tract or two or twenty
it started to hail.

settle into the stomach
settle into impression
see what a mole sees salamander, worm hole
the heavy wet oaks
the duckweed
we are still there you know.
the tissue of the slough.
the invaginate
behind the absence, anyway,
the absence of countless pictures,
the argument of nothing actually nothings.

3

diamonds face of a friend

there are diamonds in bodies
the passages and passing
to bring only the colorless light
in a thing.

there are those who cut apart the earth,
to hold them up as children,
who work for the desire of the made world.

the diamond is not an eye
it is the lens of sight.

a breeze blown diamond
a breeze blows through a diamond
. . .

now the suppression of silence
is the overfolding silence
pain
the lover is vulgar
the friend divine.

the friend is the face of the imagination
the lover the anguish of arteries.

the face goes down in the water
the lover passing through the eyes
the hands follow the lover's passage
...

no, do not be surprised
obstructed by gifts
wanted by the anemia of the vulgar.

a hand grasp, a diamond
names it
fatigue.

it grasps a diamond
and passes it through the tract,
the face of the friend
a dinner of diamonds
set up in sun salt crystals
cresticular face
facing
...

one lives to tend to
the vulgar and default
circuit of wounds
that draw vulgar,
that drinks the earth,
the spills of earth in cotton…
as when someone swims in a river
or a pond.

so where are you there then?
it takes so much,
to face the cloudy sight
the clouds in sight
and night works its way
through the diamond-eyed friends.

I came from vulgar slime,
and born to bury earth in it
to reach the face I kiss
where breath moves about mouths.
…

pathos generate degenerate
pathos logos
dynamic of a love letter
bloodletters.
and folds by silence, is folded by silence
silence folds over
crestings.

invaginate silence

in vaginate silence
walking away
I was the face
of a thought
of a grasp
but not a face
haunted by vulgarity
of a stem
of a slug.

you are there still
and all over
folded over and over
the laundry on the shelf
as if the days I have thought to open.
do not be surprised
there is no such thing as 10
it has to be made
and is among so many missed things.

the richness, the three breaths of a body
earthenware, what one should call it
the cast light
on your face
and the red ember.
demand love
and the hand changing your face
the blossom of your face
the vulgar arteries.

confection, is the sweatness
as for him, sitting among accumulate of rings,
as seeing a jar without a lid,
as the light, a blue day, spring
veiled by a curtain.
the face of the friend is not yet turned toward.
sitting among the rings,
as the sun rolls down one ring to another,
the ten rings of the jar?

you won't know.
and I will always miss you.
one cannot walk on a tract.
when holes open,
and take part in the confidence of a stride.

one can be audacious.
you are audacious like a rubber ball
stuck in the jar's mouth.
I am where you choose to leave me
as if memories were somehow
not signs of necrosis
of a love at any rate, that is as radical as, say, a
carcinogen
...

as for the confidence,
the life that is made in silence,
I would walk on you
the earth
and find myself
my mouths
full of its immaculation.

the human face expresses forms
from the blackness of matter
to the contours of forms on faces
the counters of forms in mind
glisten in faces
the glisten in faces
is the form of terrestrial imagination
its ocean blackness of matter
its form faces and obfuscation and glistening
contours and counters

the gulls lift up and draw faces and letters
the word has nervous periphery

you smiled at me in the shape of my heart
I breathe as wings beat, lungs of the wings

terrestrial imagination
is spirational

hostilius was humorous

there it leaves
and I swam up
into your arms
into your blood

no longer lingering
watching for a letter
vacant

the miserable truth
of anywhere is always ready
to appear

and as it comes through
in all the through-running moments
with bloodly cacaophony, when you coughing in my hand
set phlegm into my palm
that was the last heat I felt from you
it sat on the tissue, little runs of blood in it

I left you there
and bled all over your headstones
a 'grammy' my first amusement
I remember the infinite
…

a poem is a museum
where earthly things are put in constellation
to say what was the figures we never assigned letters
it is a language tomb
of the undead peon

please, in the halls, and in all modern pressure
do not invite me there again.

no poem is amusing
no life is precious
without tasting a body
but that sleeping guard, by the giant stone
tells me more than 2500 words.

do you mind, given your earliest morning stare
captured the softness in my spine
that stare that started late at night,
do you mind me
do we take it seriously enough?

I am in love, all day
and the stones passing
in the nursing home
a coin in a slot machine.

I am in love all day and
that means I will before,
you unite a breath to a thought
have that kiss
and let go.
...

Decius was killed with his son
they fought for the old gods
the gods that own our love
versus other gods, such as, barbarians
christian gods god and so
plotinus
sought to govern the double mouth
of the bloodletters, barbarians, old goats, the four humors.

the hall
was filling with sun
and the light made the eyes gleam
they began to make their laws
and killed
hostilius to humor his father

fistula

mother
a language is sap
the trees are morons

the stars pour from maple trees
full of fireflies

songs are gourged on the stripped branches
fat birds bloated from summer rotting
their chest cavities were abnormal

it was never a question of 'why' but merely why.
as a sentence bone in a wing
hollow
as if impaled, really, not really
as if these dead birds, with their wings
comb clouds of slate

as if I am still looking into the sky
as if it is fifty degrees
as if you were there with me

as if my fathers finally pulled themselves up
from black mud,
as if you could really be that face
that disintegrates you.

the poet without arms is a hopeless poet.
the hope of the poet is to use the arms.
and the engine of his palms.
to hold a diamond lens.

as if Orior Oriens appears in the mud
with my fathers
giving birth to one son
Occido: in the new end of the world

she does, will, showed up
showered mud with blood
planted Occido in the loom
in the loon's curling coil sound
...

or poured my coffee one day
smuggled a kiss from my expression
simply, stupidly
wanted a kiss
and rather, or certain
taste is the cumulation of the three breaths of the body.

plotinus called for this city of philosophers
campagna.
it was never funded
the poem is its best
columnal principle
at the base of the groin the hopeless poets
with their palms and their arms
write with a pen

and so humorous gushing birth day after day.
rather, the campaign of poems
and the force of language moves the flag
...

puppy bird and the phlegm partridge

as if
the puppy bird emerges
a boy rides on its back

absence rides in his eyes
a boy emerges

the taxi stand
you are sitting there giving birth
the absence in vertabrae
the stren, strenuous

you were there again today
in a red dress, maybe
purple, red in the night, purple in the early morning
you were there
I sat there too
I came back and sat there
with all the birds
at noon.

mind you
the rings I draw to that bench
and the absence that breaks each ring
mind you?
my mouth on your legs
or my coins in your belly?
...

home is not the answer
the children play
the print of the lens
they play it in their movements
the dyad saying it so

the loom is full of abscenery
because they play
the child is the memory
the child is justice
the child
dressed in sanguine dress
in the black of a phlegm partridge

Amazing blossom

an amazing blossom
a gut flower

drawn by?
blossom, thetherings, some mental net?

sexless roar, anxiety
a backstabber, an opportunist?

fat rain on the window
lit by street light like static.

recall: the sun penetrates drops
a crown inside, each drop
rolls through,
the shit and mud
on a barn door.
...

rippled apart from inside
light breaks contours.

  standing in front
the window man stands
and by waking by night by passes by
  directionless hiway.
lights of traffic lights
  esophagus, lighted fistula.

  smelt fumes,
waking murk non cosmic,
  suns rolls dark droplets,
of a hiway.
progressive metabolism.

a gut floweringing
hits before sound ever appears
every mind,
mind his hid reflection.
there watching traffic reflection
breaks up
dirt streaks dried drop light reflect
break off.

a stomach crown, sexless oblivion?
nucleus of contemporary freedom?
rub the mouth
against the glass
ghost lips drop
  glassy kids face
smashy nose.
...

Don't think i like a call
in the middle of the night.
No song, vomiting behind the eyes.
Depleted arms.
lying there moving nothing thinking about looking out at
The rest of the day for months,
Feeling hands blooming,
in my stomach.

Awake again,
fingertips dipped in stars or drops or lights

Yet this drop of water
the grey matter of dirt and shit
On the barn door.
With the sun in it, still shines.
as with the creatures in the stalls
the hot milk of a cow
six fingered cat
the half-shank corn knife.
or fly shit piled up that turned the light bulbs brown
tobacco lighting.
he was there too, walked beans with me
as a vapor.
my hands gripping stalks
wore the old boots of an old man

burned up young feet
pulled horseweed, buttonweed
the towers that brushed the blue day
burned up my hands
lived in basements

here then in the window
  stomach pulls out its roots
it is raining
in a reflection
...

drawn to
now in the morning
the deep pull
opens to a hole
 in the earth
opens
  the chest
lying here
feeling
chest center
empty
ribs are not handles
  cannot pull away,
pouring through the floor
indifference is not the
answer
liquifying
  thoughts wash away in it

ἀποφθέγγομαι

Ap·o·thegm(s) of poetry and science

Before Bachelard, before many before him, the quotidian and scientific status of objects was more a value that moved rather than the migration of movement into a concept – today we are moved by established concepts, and what about their fissures?

We know from the Milesian school through Plotinus, before the Greeks were *utterances,* meant by "that," by the tongues of inheritors who licked up millions of words, with fingers stubby and fat, slim, and dirty turning pages, whom work among candle lava, thinking utterly into concept and theory, what populated and pixelated movement into concepts, what stands as *qualia-ting* flowers: that the book falls into one screen, as the One fell from movement and the thinking of movement.

Poetry operates as the instrument and mechanical innovation of falling out and in of photos. A knee to a leg, a *viol de gamba.* There will never be a hydraulic like it, as singular as your feeling crystalizes by imagination into writing, acute-like language, or “language is reason,” to follow Hamann.

The poem – well it is clear that the value of the poem remains “ex.” What is language exposed to? Imagination. And what turns out if not the written poem that the poet inspects, and is at times inspected by readers.

In fact the poem is a strong example of thinking the quotidian to the scientific object to make it quotidian again, as if cotton. We encounter poetry, and certainly it is an everyday thing. And when we invest in it, the thinking of and with it, it’s most certainly hard won and elusive. The poem is on a piece of paper. Tape is on a piece of plastic, etcetera.

Written poetry is but a fraction of the hydraulic mechanism of the pervasive, rather permeating imagination. And even as it’s fraction, what we know of, we are utterly disbursed, already acquiescingly passed away.

The poetry of the future, should there be one, if there is a future to speak of now, is the mirror and window of ruptures, the earth is written up into the world picture. Not a mirror to the woods, as if to give human language to trees and animals. In the world picture these are infused with the four causes, as the window we forget we are looking through it, to that scene, and hovering in is our face.

We are written into the "nature" according to the world picture. This picture is only one world. The truth of relationality and scientific objects stands with reality, a world of broken time and history, and finally, the liquid imagination that binds are the recreations of countless photos.

Really, what was said here?
immediate *substance or matter* abstracted
mediation *the possibility of entering in and out of a form changes*
concept *its use and social purpose* pleasure
...

Viol de Gamba

What does it mean then "to keep?" Keep what by "a trying out"? A testing one thinks. We are left to play with this string of figures called ambit, let us proceed with a gambit. A gambit or a risk, maybe a contingency waits. In a game that we test. Yet we are not plucking a string as much as bending by a bow. We do not mean *vis* or *violatus*, not to violate or break. If to release this "soul disused ambit" the pawn-sphere or test of sacrifice "to gain an advantage" or a view that was an aspect of brilliance.

What I mean is an "ad-vantage" as *ad-* means "toward" in aspect. The spectator or species that sees before the object appears. And by this sacrifice of a "soul" the "spirit" is an aspect transpiring, a sacred still-life, what is sublated and killed-off, ex-spired. A tower or neck or spinal column looms but first a set of four strings sets this ambit off as a semi-colon.

First string of the team, the linemen dies of a broken neck. He crosses a *limus*. Fools – a string may break a thousand times if it makes a sound, it breaks a sound and not itself. First chair then: the viola da gamba: "viol of the leg." There is more. My legs are on the ground, one taps, the knee bends. A cello plays the sexless song, a mediation, this imagination from the genital amplifier: a sexlessness. These strings and a bow makes an aspect, an aspect of lyrics, the clime possible to the ear, inside and out of artificial body of an earthen production. A viol de gamba, the risk, is sustainable no less administered by a human player who strokes the device (yes the blue one but also a green one) and breaks a song by bending strings together, splays the soul of an ambit by each torsion of each of four strings.

Gamba means "leg" from a few languages and constitutes a constellation of parts: "hinge, calf, hoof." It bends and breaks open the earthen being, the upper stop. It comes from the body into the wooden body as a sound. Early prosthetic transpiration once merely notational "music," but it was written, and thus, it was imagined, that is, imaged.

This orchestration is a testing of the device to bend its strings. From Latin gamba means various things. And in English its other uses resonate.

other poems or
chromoromance

chromoromantish

inringin
  eternal summer
the sea chewed

a poem births its future
a configured sense an untruth
the-writi~~ng~~-splice-variegates-*chromos*

the poem's vanity
a tunnel in its vision
                                      /

the poem's point
of view
understands

irrepressible
orthodoxy
without
pretense:
                    /

the poem dilates twice to a choraling
chro-mo-ro-man-tic-ism.

everyday the sidewalk is full of
themthe flower toroids, mock;
the capillaries flushing,

and all eyes right now flush out the light of thought
in depth,
the ear drums tap out
mutant colors
on sound

on this table,
with my breakfast.

walking down the sidewalk
to buy cigarettes.
the sidewalk is
full of *receptacles.*

hopscotch goes these kids about
chora poematics.
the first mouth called second gives rise to
jumps about jumps
jumpers jumping off heads of other jumpers

jumping through each
into a sexless, phonoromatic.

it hardly matters, it matters on a quarter note
the quarter note of the poem
dilate mispe-late.
palliate
. . .

chromoromancer

Hamann, Bradley

what is it, if not the poet's city
that we never occupy?
and focus
always preoccupies
every foot fall
in every page
and everessence of a
lettered passage
though hand gestures
— for example —
my body when running

when wind
lays green lines horizontal
shone emerald, wax coating, a near wind
will blue has blown — blows
rhembo

up the hillside
wind carves a home in
self-pup-ous-lish
cloudlings
lingers at ground level, wind shaves the pond
windsoaked stems
the long claws of some ancient bird

no shame is essence
high towers are the ground level
of the poet's city
the poet sleeps in
the tower's basement
sleeps inoutside
windows
in that air

his-she comet
a head and spine
impregnating glass

she-his sits between
iron bars
of the fortress

chromoromance
...

quotidian phone

but my face is smug,
a mugshot canister
smuggled in
thighs the phone sits upon

the phone sits in quotidianity
I don't understand
the flowers and plates,
the gold laced high ceiling
the plates glint with cutlery
faces feed politely

life wastes on its own
and what grows beneath it.
that scene ... is obscure if not at first
ob scene

why do we hang ourselves
as if suspended from the earth
in dreams?

what does the quote do if not that
hang around
how many quotidian phones quote breath
exchanged for breadth

the richest people slice up and down
with stares
a faceless beef cow
whose balls were cut off
skin torn off
bled rendered

they lay it on the table, as if it was a well cooked tree
trunk
some slave saws it for them
in the bubbles of blood, the plates are empty and glint
with cutlery

...

wet father photo

drenched photo

the incredible grip of a tree
          a treereflects all thought
the slow throbbing trunk
in the squeeze of soil
the blackends of fleshy life,
the blackveins of being
the incredible truth
flesh has no place
yet thought
flesh place of thought
the only thought

in grasses
the thighs of
grassy hills
in bones sun beams
spread out
tucked under
tree beltlines

i do know something
that in life, this life
i stumble into absences
and all these things happen.

the dead fathers in an absence appear
not sure —
if these faces were looking
this way
if they spoke
my way

outlines, white outlines —
a scene of this father
speaking in
an old video tape
across that wood fence,
a field crumpled by
sun, woods,
cut by the outline of a wooden fence
there
feet in lush weeds
holding mother baby
stop by the back of his head, ear
and hear no voice
novice bonds
in bones outline

an absence

is a moment to define, perhaps
your self fathers,
live their statements
we'd call experience.

absence is the place we hold
we hold hands
sweet face, still face
soft
eyes round slate
i love you perhaps
you want to be a man
to get out of a young face
as i have always tried
i cannot get rid of its shape
absence holds it
and has a way of keeping it ahead
of judgment

did you know
your young face was never mine?
and the absence that you hold is my sense
that is where love is
all around you.

i hope it was beautiful for you
when you went
up
became an eagle

or feather fibers
have instinct for
aer
he
arche arms back

your chest anneal, an eagle

what mouth of a che st
the color a mute like yellow
  sound a solar flare

was morning when
this sea became the air
was sundown when
'where is earth' was asked
It was pulled off in the passing sun

if sea became aer
was because rain
came from grounded clouds

and this blue ribbon
was morning when it came
to build

these blue ribbons painted on
high rise over there layers of yous
smearely blue shirted men smile at the face of whose
question is his expression

when the sea became the air
green leaves melted
red branches

i keep
moving
through where been
i was moving even

then uneven
doubt knots could ex-press it
but your hands are sized
by afghans you left

in the end of your mind;

i keep moving

those stars in my head
threads my mind
keeps
with the size of moving
the size of my moving

my footings still moving
still slowly
still crushing
back
from a stop
crouch and let your knees see.

i keep moving in your moving
ab dictate
ob vious
away from the declaration
means before the way

(dont worry iloveyou)

that butter life of your life
as my moving
time makes us differently the same.

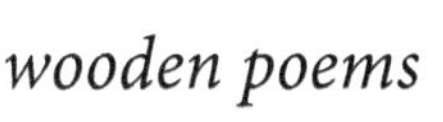

strip club museum

these dancers
dance
in dark forums
in slung blue-purple
fall from Orion's
arms
in butterflied
ohm's law land
of light

crushed up
fresh tin chips
speckles
fallen from
the silk
of aboral
tentus

leapt up
pe pole
these
aboreal legs
scissors open
a butterflied
declench clench

anarbor eye
on
lathe

light sun in the tree is law
'sun is in the trees now'
in the arbor grove
sun unspun cotton

these tin chips
in purple-blue light
attach to the eyelens

holding firm virgin
abides the glint
print
sight
to sound
force
voice living statues

in dark forums
grief
grasps
a cooing mouth
ear is still
a cooing mouth
still in the coo
  vacancy
reminds me
I am alone

birdsbeak

how far does one go
did I appear through

a birds knifebeak? instancizations of
i t s pecker pensil
  puncturer beak pencil of weather

pencil weather
 a loose tit of graphite,
uncountable noun verbarium
problem water and color
  of medium

faces emerge from the population of a word

as a bird has a flag
on each wing
it's color songwater

a birds head
in my hand
birdeye my figurenails

the eyes of the bird
are erasers
  obsidian eraser pools
contractive apertures in meltfleshed sidewalkers

bird's eyes are
one straight rod
the rod hangs
the bird in the air
pours through the fistula
waterweather sky
  makes clouds

afternoon
diapers hang
some smoky dusk orange
spurt yolk
uncurls like a seed in diaperish skylines

pensil pecker breaks its shell
breaks,
silt from the
knifebeak black yogurt of sight in its song

bird enthrones
the three flight
gem of the throne
in its sight

its regality, span of history
the flags of wings
flutters on
its perch
expands them
sitting there
retracts wings
flagpole
birds eye

faculty in words

an occasion of letters…
the face of a poem comes from the population in its words.

on occasion I get
a notion about
my sense of
location in reference
to
walking, say,
in my own house.

I get a sense about others.
I wear the glimmer of
anxious blooms
ancient blooms and   think about
an archive

I also wonder what history looks at me.
collisions of the wide
world, the making world
expanding
i drawn to time lapse
video typed image —
what ills me is this referent.

One can figure out a letter-
a letter and the letter.
what is supposed about letters?
a letter is supposed as
premium photographeme
in fact, what it captures
is something about silence
among participants, standing out.
The letter, say D or B or Z,
the snowflake of an image is the brilliant face

Perception is durable and limited by the newness of
the way of
images.
In poems, in the words
images are snowing, a snowingness.

Acute pressure
the problems of privileged
eyes. it is the fact of focus
What would eyes ever point to?
In their center, it is always a
taking hole.
Yet thought seems
  pointing out
and thought the images
of snowing.

Maybe. For now I am thinking
about all that stands out of the
letter, a letter I have yet to
send.

Tonight, by the train tracks
enough moisture that steel is smelt
and iron, in particular iron,
iron in the air
a cold fire of snow
this is a snowing of the laid rail.
Poems and pages, what is it that
has a tactility then, if only a
musty book?

I think the poems I had
written, worked among a
snow fall
and chased it.

For one reason or another
I am thinking about this
feeling depth,
a depth that
seems to feel my thinking.
A depth without a center, not too different from
        trying to touch the unsheathed eye with a finger
a depth without silence.
This depth is the core of a snow
fall, all snow goes
never in
too
it.
and it is only in here.
This is the pressure behind
The paradox of eye sight That
one thinks looks out.

The truth may say
we have seen only nothing
yet.
poetry has no place in the world
that makes out looking the
beginning of thought.

poetry only snows in the ban
of sight.
eyes are empty cups, like
soil in fact the fat of soil.
water fills them, and, eventually
drowns the feeble believer.
This is why poets make
ships
in a drowned world of many
sites – sights, in a tourist
world, the arc of the self.
  why the beasts with swollen balls, breaks fur, as if a
fire
and
fruits of the pressured
and
freezing sea speak to a poet
life, finds a geo form

and where letters originate.
in the pounding of the bulls horns

in the light starved snow of impossible depth.

the sea is full of disintegrations
snow is the unfrozen mirror a logic
soilbrittle archive too
in would a mirror tell
eyes the truth about outward
stabbings
and vacant thought
  could be, for now,
  sight into its
resource,
the thought of a hog's blue eyes.
This is what it means, only briefly,
to catch oneself walking
and to struggle about letters.

Black Veins

This figure faces,
apothegmatics.
And the regime of minding poetry
is a built hall.
built hall full of chairs.
Of chairs, are wooden like birch.
And like birch they are elbows.
And like elbows they are knees.
As much as an arm is a leg,
the heart the logic of caves,
the rib cage interstate system.
The hall full of mouths mouths that draw up aural
cape-ability,
what crowns the assemblage,
what tilts the flag is the everydayness of breathing.

as much a river washes invisible hands
as much a river mocks the mouths in the hall
as much it claps abeyance
as much the wood plank creeks
the tree claps back
the sun draws / lips on
the handless washing of the river
as much the dead otter I swam by
as much the glass bottle from 1970 something with
the hand that threw it
hands washed in the river that tells you that
the river tells now under ice
the small bluffs
the stone heart
dumps over the water
and the fat august air *retinized*

Black Veins, is a matter of 'taking someone at their word'. When reading 'someone at their word' we already take words

you will be fine
you have not lost anything
to fix on loss;
  to miss what emerges
to think about loss;
  has nothing to do with;
  the sun that irises
the memor of what is gone.

just a wooven glass and aspects now of deposits
then minerals in water in soil.
the trees churned to asphault
say as a vine that grapples the oak,
turns bloody in fall
  a period, the sun draining down through the eye dia
and runs down the trunk
pump the sun
the whole story of slugs and worms and birds dung that
                                        they are and so on
when winter gives its cancer
the woods taught me
as a kid as a man as kind kinder kerning thought
things emerge and devour each other in obspaces.
vines grapple the oak tree, parts the soil oars into mud
                                                        slown
then oak trees felllen already
roots cavities holes in the mud
bugs and black mud devour the oak trunk, the houses
living human life is like that sinkhole of obliteration
life like memor
problem is that we think it inblinking memor
unique to us and the nature of our pain
what we've made into glass we'ave
our pain and nature into the cosmons
fighting against the ob in the hostwords vessels

forget the caravels, the sloops, galleys
I affirm the nature of this life as some that is spreadopen
one regardless of what I think about its fact
…

that is the same thing however
when the ob of your voice
is death
pushing into the words
spreading them theme openly
negenly
the thinking in my mind in the spreadin of y/our
voice in a word
spread the loven heat of speech why don't you?
...

throw your breath in my thought one more time
or I am a foam cup in the bay may be
with the sick ducks
foam and algae

throw my oar tongue
in your
mouth one more time
not for the memor moment only
not for when it crystalizes
rather
for the fact it does not have to
reaches it waves me in my shot
commands it relentlessness
…

you (he) speak like machine guns
so shut the fuck up?
and shoot one.
...

don't accuse pleaseme
don't accuse; give me a fetish;
I love shotguns
kill birds and eat them
kill fowl and tear them
into a meal, near raw fowl.
all kills are done in the
"when the ob of your voice
is death
pushing into the words
spreading them theme openly
negenly"

pity that poems are just like that
each shot in the air a poem scheme
most of the poems are like that

μετεμψύχωσις

(Certainly we will only proliferate vacancies in answering, rather responding to what we consider to be missing. In that regard what is missing is demanded by an irreversible material accumulation and its "explosions" or releases. What is released from historical-material tension if not *tendency*; a tension and tendency to rupture, a tendency of reflex and movement, what we otherwise think we are discovering as openings in knowledge? The professional academic certainly claims the latter, I'd like to think this an ecology of epistemology that the poet, and only the poet offers an ethos for, of which the metaphysics older than the antiquated and exhausted definitions of it no longer grasp, that the metaphysics I speak of will ethically endure as metabolic relation for the sustaining of the human imagination as the most precious resource in the universe. For now we are in text soaking them with nothing but echoes, and the secrets of the nothing in echoing is perhaps an *area* or scope that passes through the stylus of the poetic ex-. So goes our share in furthering definitions, that so-called voice of the text which constructs the tonality of the built world, or the injection of intelligence from the primordial earth into the synthetic. No less in relation to our survival as thinking humans this is the mouth-to-mouth resuscitation of a question and not an arrival: what must be human, or what must have been human, and what becomes human? To find the queerness of metempsychosis, or what it means to migrate through historical material, what it means to come up through ruptures, to pass through the glass canals of the screen that is less and less a fiction of the mind and corrupts the historical as it creates its intelligence. To find the echo and to enlarge it, its vision of sound, its kinetic net. In this way metempsychosis is not merely a coming to terms, as in a form of life in its third trimester, it means the singly of the many through the wordiness of terminal ports, the verb is always of the porous sentence. It is the arrangement with it today that leads us to a conviction about what it means to publish a book, and what those sentences, fragments mean within it as an echo, and what one demands of scope of a reader who echoes by whatever reason they chose, the propagation of its claim, of the life and its copies. It means precisely what the poem has achieved and remains to teach us as a subject of study – in both "the poetic subject" of study, and the poetic of subjectivity.)

CONTENTS

The photographic composition is the field of pure evidence. It becomes the structuring element offering the possibility of a form, or complex of forms, multiplying the results of geometry to infinity. Water, concrete, dust, mud, metal: a nebulous material mist depicted as a concrete event. (In these photographs there is nothing but the call of forms organized as vehicles of a regression into the world).

– Marco Mazzi

www.ingramcontent.com/pod-product-compliance
Lightning Source LLC
La Vergne TN
LVHW090520110826
845146LV00003B/933